HELLO FELLOW CRAFTER!

This short book is designed to take you by the hand and lead you through the process to having your own successful craft stall at a fair or market.

It is not a magic wand (sorry) and it doesn't do the work for you (sorry again!), but it does give you lots of tips and practical advice to help you to have the most successful craft stall possible.

You can absolutely start selling at craft fairs without any help from me... but I have been where you are now and have learned the lessons the hard way, so why not take advantage of someone else doing the leg work and learn from my experience?

WHO IS THIS BOOK FOR?

Did you start crafting during lockdown?
Have you always loved making things?
Do family and friends say "You should sell those?"
Have you made items as presents.
Do you wonder if anyone else would buy what you make?

If you recognised yourself in any (or all) of those questions, then this book is for you. Wondering 'what if...' is the start of your journey.

You do have to put some work in though. Sorry.

If you really want to succeed at selling your crafts, then you have to be honest with yourself and look at what you make with a critical eye. You need to use this book. Write in it; highlight things and generally make it your own. I can give you all the information, but you need to apply it to **your** situation and **your** craft.

Having said all that...you also need to have fun! If it's not fun, then stop. If it is making you stressed, then stop. Selling your crafts makes you part of a crafting community that is awesome.

Right, enough of that....let's get on....

What do you make?

OK, let's start at the very beginning. Which, I am told, is a very good place to start!

The first thing you need to think about is 'What do you make?' I am assuming, for the purposes of this training that you already have a product that you enjoy making and you would like to sell at craft fairs. We need to look at four separate aspects to answer this question comprehensively and in a way that will mean that you can go forwards to have a successful selling experience. I will go into each of these in more detail.

The four sections are:

- IS IT GOOD ENOUGH?
- IS ANYONE ELSE SELLING IT?
- HOW EASY IS IT TO MAKE?
- IS IT FINANCIALLY VIABLE?

Let's get started...

IS IT GOOD ENOUGH?

Up until now, you may have just sold to friends and family, or even just had friends and family telling you that "You should sell those". I'm here to be the voice of reason. I don't want to be mean, and I certainly don't want to discourage you, but you do need to take a step back and look at your product with a critical and impartial eye.

Look at your products as if you are seeing them for the first time (hard, I know, but give it a go). Inspect the finish that you have achieved. Are there loose threads that haven't been run in? Are there small difficult-to-get-to sections where you haven't quite reached with the paint brush? Are all the lines straight and the cuts parallel? Have you used the cheapest wool that splits when you stitch it together? You get the idea. Depending on what your product is; look carefully and closely at the finish that you have achieved. Be totally honest with yourself – could it be improved? If your answer is a begrudging 'yes', then spend some time tweaking and polishing and then do this exercise again. Does that make the finished product better?

Depending on what your product is, you will also need to test it out. If you have made washable face wipes, do the colours run when they are washed? Do they actually work well to remove make-up while feeling soft on your skin? If you are making candles; is the length of wick right or do they smoke when you blow them out? You need to make absolutely sure that your items are fit for purpose. You eventually want to have repeat customers and referrals, so you need to make sure from an early stage that your product really does what it says on the tin.

This is also a stage where you can adapt products and refine them. Don't simply dismiss it if something is not quite right.

Try swapping to slightly higher quality yarn, putting a washer on every screw hole or adding an under-glaze for brighter colours. You can also add user information. Telling customers to 'wash at 30°' is fine, if you know that washing them at a higher temperature will damage the finish.

In this testing and refining stage, you need to keep and use your items for a good few weeks. I always try to allow a month for new products so that I can see what the wear is like, but it obviously depends on what you are making. You may think this is unnecessary if you are painting artwork to hang, for example, but you will still need to know whether you need to advise it being hung out of direct sunlight etc.

Next you need to find some impartial opinions. This can be more difficult than you would think! If you have a brutally honest friend or family member, then start there, but they usually just want to be kind and encouraging. Facebook groups can be useful here. If you are a member of a local crafting group (which is a very good thing to be for many reasons), you will often see crafters trying out new products and asking for feedback. You may get some. In my experience, however, people don't want to be seen as unkind and will often only tell you the positives. That's great, of course, but at this stage you need to know all the opinions.

The obvious way to find out opinions is at your first sale. People will either buy...or not. You will also hear lots of opinions on your products throughout the day. My job here is to make that as positive an experience as it can be. At the end of the day, look at your products, be happy that they are the best quality they can be and ask yourself one question:

"If I saw this at a craft fair, would I stop to look and potentially buy one?"

IS ANYONE ELSE SELLING IT?

You may think that you need to find something that no-one else is selling and something that is completely unique to you. The truth is that basically, if you thought of it, so did someone else! This is not a bad thing. The fact that there are other people out there selling similar items to you, just means that there is a market for those products. If no-one is selling it, then it probably means no-one wants it. There are obviously some exceptions. If you were the first person to make enormous hair bows, then you would have started a huge trend! Generally, though, for us mere mortals, there is going to be someone else out there selling something similar to what we make.

This does not mean that the USP that everyone goes on about is not important. USP stands for Unique Selling Point and is the thing about your products that makes you different. It may be as simple as only using eco-friendly bamboo in your makes, only using shades of blue, or even having a distinctive box that sets your packaging apart from others. This is not essential, but it's good to have so that people can refer to you as "The one that makes the square candles" or whatever your equivalent is.

The next question to ask yourself is "Is there a need for this?" The best and easiest way of working this out is to go on Pinterest and type in the name of your product. Be as specific as you can. Instead of 'Handmade dog collars', go for 'Personalised handmade dog collars', for example. This will show you if there is a need for your product. It can also give you more ideas and get your creative juices flowing. Just remember; it's brilliant to be inspired by others, but it's not okay to just copy.

Okay, now I want to give you a bit of homework. I would like you to find 5 other businesses that make and sell the same (or similar) products to you. They could be local to you and people you know or have seen at craft fairs; they could be people you have just found on Pinterest or on Instagram or simply businesses that pop up when you put in a Google search. They don't need to be an exact match for your business, but similar in some way.

This is your chance to see how other similar businesses sell their products. They may have multi-buys that are very popular or aim their product at a specific type of person that you haven't thought of. You can also start to get a feel for the realistic pricing of your products. You will need to consider things like: different ingredients, if there is P&P included and so on, but it will give you a basic idea of where to pitch your prices.

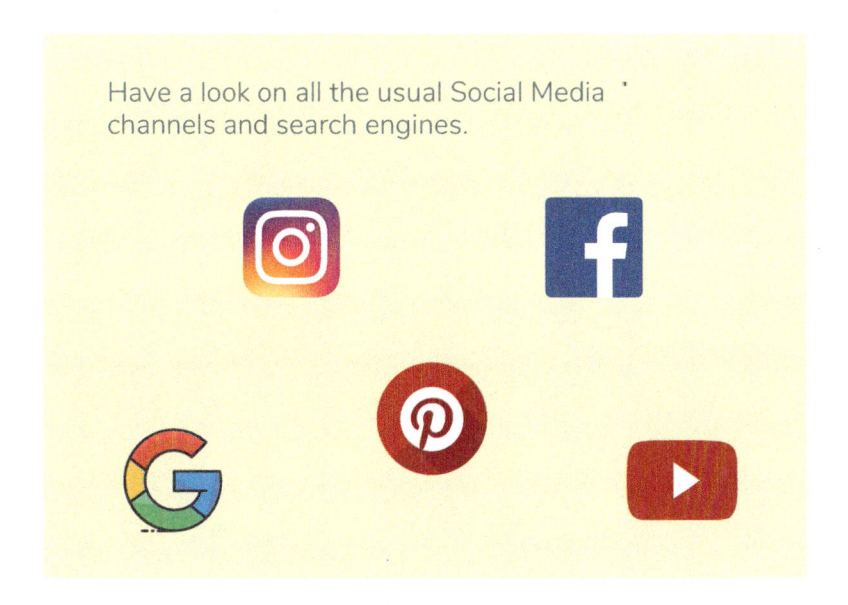

Have a look on all the usual Social Media channels and search engines.

HOW EASY IS IT TO MAKE?

This is an interesting question because, presumably, you enjoy making your product which is why you want to carry on. You have now checked that you haven't fallen into the trap of making something you enjoy making rather than something that people will actually buy, so you need to look at the practicalities.

Firstly, you do need to actually enjoy making your product. If you start to sell lots, which, let's face it, is what you are hoping for, then you will also need to make lots. Can you see yourself making your product long term or trying to get lots finished for a deadline? If the answer is 'no' then you need to rethink now. Most of us have one part of the process that we don't really look forward to. If you knit, it might be sewing in all the ends, if you make wax melts, it might be thoroughly cleaning down the equipment before changing colours. Whatever it is, think about how much you hate it in the grand scheme of things. At the moment, it's fine, you can put up with it, but if you were making more, would it get you down? There are many ways round this. You can do a little of the worst job before you start each session so it gets done first, you could put your favourite music or podcast on and get it all done in one go. It may sound trivial now, but it's worth thinking about before you start.

Next, I would like you to see if you could streamline any of your processes. This sounds very grand, but for you (and me), the best way to do this is to batch the jobs. This simply means doing all of the same bits of the process at the same time – very technical!! If you are making wooden bedroom signs, you might make ten at once. You could cut ten, then sand ten, then paint ten, then varnish ten, then add the names. This would be much more efficient in terms of time than making each one from start to finish before starting the next. This leads me nicely on to...

Do you have a designated area for crafting? Most of us are squished on the dining room table, in the back bedroom or with a plug-in heater in the shed. That's fine and it works. You do, however, need to think about the available space that you have. If you have to tidy up after every making session so that the family can eat breakfast tomorrow, then having storage is key. You need to think about storage for products that are mid-make (especially if you are batching) as well as somewhere to compile stock before a sale.

It is no secret to any of my friends or family that I love a list. You need to embrace the list too. Making sure that you know exactly where your items are is key to making the most of your crafting time. Always putting things away properly and in the same place may seem a pain at the time, but I promise you, it really helps in the long run. I will come back to this later. Also, a quick top tip is to keep a little notebook with your making things so you can make a note of exactly where you got up to last time you worked on it. This will help to keep you sane despite family interruptions – I speak from experience!

The last thing to think about in this section is your skill level. Is there anything you need to work on or learn to help with your making? Looking back at the 'Is this good enough? section; did you identify anything that needs work now? It could be that you just need to follow a YouTube tutorial (what did we do before YouTube?) and then practice, or it could be that you need to invest in a little bit of kit (e.g. better tile cutters) or maybe even learn from a pro (ask your family for a day making wicker hurdles for your next birthday present). Whatever it is, sort it out now.

IS IT FINANCIALLY VIABLE?

The bottom line for this is obviously "Can I sell this for more than it costs to make?" There is, however, slightly more to it that that. Sorry!

Firstly, you need to decide why you want to sell your products. There could be many reasons. You may want to make a little bit of money for charity, you might have a huge stash of beads that you just want to use up and get your money back on, or you might just want to try a new skill.

We will come back to your reasons for selling in a moment. First let's look at the costs.

Costs are more involved than you might think. There are the obvious expenses of the raw materials that you use, but there is also any training you have paid for, any display equipment you have bought alongside the cost of the table at your craft fair. Factoring the time you take to create your products into the equation is a huge issue in itself and not one that I want to go in here (there is just too much to say), but you do need to give a little thought to whether you want to get paid for your time as well.

Right, back to your reasons for selling...

"I enjoy making and just want to give it a go" In this instance, go for it! You do however, still need a grasp of the basic costs. It's all very well wanting to 'have a go at a craft fair', but you do want to at least break even, and preferably make a little bit of profit!

"I'd like to make enough to supplement my income" Now the costs become more important as you want to continue selling and you have a goal in mind. It really helps to have a specific goal written down. Work out how much you need and what it is for. You'd be surprised at how it focusses you.

"I'd like to replace my income and quit my job" This is a more long-term goal and there is nothing to say that you can't work your way through all three of these options. For this to work, though, you need to have a very clear handle on all of your income and outgoings from the start. This may be where you want to end up, but for now we will concentrate on that very first craft fair. Who knows where it may lead!

YOUR TURN:

What do you make?

This section is for you to do some work to apply what you have learned to your own situation. Take some time to fill in each part - it will really help you focus on your next steps.

IS IT IT GOOD ENOUGH?

1. Who can I ask to give me an honest opinion of my products?

1. Family:

2. Friends:

3. Groups:

2. Which products will I focus on? Pick your 'top' 3

Product 1:

Product 2:

Product 3:

3. How will I test out each product?

Product 1:

Product 2:

Product 3:

4. How long will I need for this process?

5. What actions do I need to take? e.g. YouTube video, training, better equipment...

Where do I sell?

Now that you have made some decisions, and maybe, faced some difficult truths (sorry!) about what to sell, it's time to think about where to sell.

Don't expect to get this right straight away. You will have some 'bad' sales days at the start. I'm afraid we all do. You just need to look at the basics and check that you are in the best place possible for you. This may take a little trial and error, but if you follow these simple pointers, you will have the best possible chance of striking gold (or at least copper) from the start.

I have split this into 6 easy to digest sections:

- **LOOK AT WHAT IS ALREADY BEING SOLD THERE**
- **START SMALL**
- **WHAT IS PROVIDED BY THE ORGANISERS?**
- **WHAT ARE THE TERMS AND CONDITIONS?**
- **LOCATION, LOCATION, LOCATION**
- **INDOOR VERSUS OUTDOOR**

LOOK AT WHAT IS ALREADY BEING SOLD THERE

This may seem obvious, but you would be surprised at how many people miss this step out. If possible, go and visit the venue before the sale. If it is a regular fair or market, then go along while it is in full swing and get a 'feel' for the place. If that is not possible, you can pick up some clues from looking at event photos (Facebook pages are good for this) or talking to people who have sold there in the past.

I would say that there are three main strategies here:

- Talk to the vendors. If you can, chat to the stallholders and see whether they sell there regularly (a good sign) and if they are happy with the set up. I would be totally up-front about this and say that you are thinking about applying for a stall. You will find that 99% of stallholders are happy to chat to you and welcome you to their midst. You will also find that they are very honest about the pros and cons of a particular venue. One note of caution though; there will always be one stallholder who is never happy no matter what, so don't believe everything you hear!

- Take a general overview of the venue. As you approach, is there signage to say where to go? Does it look welcoming and is there a buzz around the room. You will find some venues that are deathly quiet. There is nothing more off-putting for a customer than walking in to a quiet room where everyone looks at you and no-one speaks. You are obviously interested in how busy it is, but all fairs have a lull when it gets quieter, so be aware of that. Make sure to notice if the stallholders are chatting to each other. Friendly and chatty sellers make for a good atmosphere where you will be welcomed and where people are more likely to buy.

- Finally, look at what is for sale. You are now attuned to 'good quality' produce from taking a good hard look at your own. Apply that knowledge to what you see being sold. Would you be happy to be grouped with the quality that is available? Look at the prices that are being charged. It will give you a good idea about where to pitch your own if you were to sell at that venue. This could be a good thing...or not, but better to know beforehand. Looking at how stalls are laid out can give you ideas for your own stall (we will come back to that later), both in a positive "Wow, that's a great idea" way, and also in a not so positive "Oh, you can't really see the things at the back" kind of way. Both are valuable to you.

One last point about looking at what is already sold is to look for items that are similar to yours. You can get a wealth of information from that. Look at pricing, display, level of finish etc. Do not be put off if there is another stall similar to yours. It may mean that you would be unsuccessful in getting a pitch if that stall has booked first, but it also means that if they haven't booked and you do, the customers are already there looking for what you sell.

START SMALL

You don't have to aim for the sky to start with. It's very tempting to book a weekend festival pitch, but until you know the up and downs of your own particular 'stall presence', don't try to run before you can walk.

For the first couple of fairs, you need to make sure that you have realistic expectations. I'm not trying to discourage you here, just to in-still a little realism. We have all had afternoons where there are hardly any customers because it's raining hard, there has been no advertising, the hall you are in is small, dark and uninviting. We have also all had afternoons where everyone around you seems to sell, but you hardly sell anything. Do not be discouraged. The gods of the stallholder are fickle! Sometimes there is just no explanation and you just have to take it on the chin. That is much less likely to happen, however, if you have followed my simple guidelines.

Village halls are often what people first think of when they think of Craft Fairs in the UK. They are a great place to start (or stick with!) There are many advantages to village hall craft fairs.

- They usually come with a built-in supply of customers. Most of the locals will be used to attending the fairs if they are run regularly and are keen to visit.
- They are usually well run and organised; generally, by a committee and often by an organisation such as the WI. This means that they will be well advertised and signed in the local community.
- They usually supply chairs and tables for you, which is so much easier when you are just starting out.
- The cost for a table at a local craft fair is usually at a level that doesn't turn your hair white.
- There is usually a good community spirit and everyone helps each other. You will get good advice – often whether you ask for it or not.
- Finally, and most importantly, there are usually stacks of amazing homemade cakes!

Things to bear in mind about local village hall type fairs include:
- Getting there. If it is your local village; great, but check that the place you have booked isn't in the middle of nowhere.
- The age demographic. There are some villages that have thriving communities that are mainly older people. Equally, if the hall is surrounded by a brand new housing estate, you could have lots of children through the doors. Neither of these is good or bad, but you need to think about how they fit with your ideal customer.
- If you are in a rural location, bear in mind that you may not have a wifi signal. This would mean that you would not be able to use a card reader for payments. Most village halls now have their own wifi, but it can still be rather patchy at best. You know you are accepted by the other stallholders when you are let into the secret of which corner you need to stretch into to get the best signal.

Other good 'starter' venues are places such as schools or pubs. Again, you need to think about who you are aiming your products at. If you do a great range of hair accessories for less than £5, you could make a killing at a school fair. If, however, you sell watercolour landscapes for £100+, then maybe not...although I guess it would depend on the school!

Retirement villages are a fairly new addition to this list. They have sprung up all over and are often keen to support community interaction. Christmas, is an especially good time to look out for these. Be prepared for the heating to be up high!

For all of these venues; be proactive. Have a look on local websites as well as Facebook. Networking is definitely your friend. The more you chat to other stallholders, the more you will find out about local fairs and sales that will suit your products and will treat you well. 99% of stallholders will be keen to suggest other events to you once they get to know you and your style. As with most things, word of mouth recommendations are always the best and most reliable.

WHAT IS PROVIDED BY THE ORGANISERS?

This section covers the practical aspects of what is provided. We will come on to the Terms and Conditions in the next section.

Before you sign up for a stall, you need to be clear on what you will need to provide and what will be provided for you. There are all sorts of options these days, but you need to be a little wary of just going for the 'easiest' option straight away.

The most obvious things are tables and chairs. Many venues will provide these. When you are starting out, this can be a real help as you don't need to borrow or buy a table and (maybe just as importantly) you don't need to fit it in your car and lug it around when you get there. Be a little wary here, though. When I first started doing craft fairs, it was the norm to have tables provided. They were part of the deal and were the standard 6' by 2' table, which is very common in village halls across the country. Now, however, many venues have got savvy and charge extra for the use of their tables. It may only be £5 or £10, but that is money out of your pocket meaning that you will need to sell more to recoup the cost. It may be completely worth it in your situation, but it's definitely worth taking into consideration and you should always include this cost in your calculations of how much initial outlay you have had for a fair.

Just a couple of additions to this, speaking from experience: check the dimensions of your table. If you have practiced your display on a 6'x2' space and then you get a 4' square table, you will be thrown if you are just starting out. If you know before hand, you can plan for it. Also, don't assume that if you pay for a table, you will automatically get a chair! It doesn't always happen ☺

Access to an electric point (plug socket) is also now much more common as an 'added extra'. You may not require this, but if you want lights or a turntable, then it's something to consider. Personally, I would recommend battery lights to start with, if you want to use lights. Keeping it simple is best at the start (and actually as you continue too!)

If you are taking part in a WI fair (as an example), you may be lucky and be offered free hot drinks. If your booking form does not specify this, then assume you will need to take food and drink. Again, I would advise you to hold out and not give in to the temptation of what is offered for sale. Those are your profits that you are eating, no matter how delicious they are!

One other thing to check before signing up for any sale is how the event will be advertised. You will find that many organisations tell you this up-front, but for smaller fairs, it may be worth asking the question. Don't feel that you are being pushy; this is something that all organisers will have given thought to (and if they haven't, then you really need to know about it!) Hopefully, your organisers will have advertised in local magazines, in Facebook groups and on notice boards as well as having good signage up on the day directing people in. I have attended fairs in the past where advertising was pretty non-existent despite all prior assurances. It is a bad sign when there are no signs! If there is no poster on the main route to your venue, then you could be in for a quiet day. If that happens, make the most of it, chat to other stall holders and learn from the experience.

WHAT ARE THE TERMS AND CONDITIONS?

You will (or should) find all the Ts and Cs on the booking form for the venue. Some places send out separate information packs with extra details on for you. You need to make sure you read these carefully. There are a few main things to look out for:

Do you need to have Public Liability Insurance?

This is now commonplace for most craft fairs. You may find that local church fairs don't ask for it, but I wouldn't bank on it. Pretty much, if you are wanting to sell your wares publicly, then you need insurance. This covers you for things such as someone tripping over your display, something falling on their head etc. It sounds very unlikely, but it is possible. I am not going to go into the legal side of making and selling here other than to say that obviously you need to put disclaimers on things like candles (do not burn unattended) etc. I am assuming that if you are wanting to sell your product, you have looked into any legal responsibilities linked to that product. In terms of the Public Liability Insurance, you are taking the responsibility away from the venue and many venues will not let you sell without it. Don't panic! This is not difficult to get. You can do it online at any of the major insurance companies. If you Google 'Craft fair insurance', for example, you will find loads. You will also find several smaller insurance companies that specialise in craft businesses. I know this is an extra cost, but it is unavoidable and once it is paid, it's done for the year.

Are there any extra costs?

We have already talked about the hire of tables, chairs and the use of power, but this could also include parking costs. Will you have to park in a public car park? If so, how much does it cost to park all day?

Do you need to pay a deposit?

Even small fairs sometimes ask for a deposit well in advance to secure your place and then the balance nearer (or on) the day. This is fine, but it is worth asking about refunds. Obviously, the last thing you want to do is cancel, but if you did, would you get a full refund? Equally, if the venue had to cancel, would you be given a full refund then?

Not long ago, there was an outdoor weekend market close to where I live that had to cancel during the week before the event due to storms being forecast. Everyone who had paid for a stall lost all of their booking fee. It stated quite clearly in the Ts and Cs that this would happen, but many people hadn't read them very carefully. I think in future, they will read all paperwork twice – that particular event was £200 for a stall for the weekend. It was an expensive learning curve for some.

Do you need to pay for a set of fairs all in one go?

If you are signing up for several fairs at the same venue, do you need to pay for them all at the start of the year? This can work well, but you just need to be aware that there will be an outlay. Incidentally, it is always worth checking if there is a deal in this situation.

Often venues with regular Farmer's Markets, for example, want regular vendors and are willing to reward you for booking more markets by giving you a good price. 12 for the price of 10 is pretty common as it means that even if you have to miss one, you are still saving money. If you do have to miss one (e.g. for a holiday), make sure you let them know when booking.

What do you need to provide when you book?

Obviously, there will be the insurance documents, but you may also be asked for some product photos or a little bit of blurb about you, your business or why you do what you do. If this happens, it is worth spending a bit of time making sure what you send is as good as it can be. Not only will it be used in their advertising, but you will also have it there, ready for any future fairs. You should see this as a huge bonus as it means that the organisers are on top of their advertising and proactive about getting people interested in the sale.

It is worth making sure that any product photos have your logo or website/Facebook page address on them somewhere. The easier people find it to discover 'your world', the better.

I know that paperwork can feel scary when you haven't had to do it before, but the reality is much more....

this

than

this!

LOCATION, LOCATION, LOCATION

There are two main questions here:

> How far away is it?

and

> Is it a difficult journey?

Considering the distance to the venue seems like an obvious and immediate thing to do and in some ways it is. If you live in Edinburgh, you would not be thinking to drive down to Plymouth for a village craft fair. Having said that, if you lived in Birmingham, you may consider selling at a weekend festival in Devon. It all depends on the costs. Firstly, do you have your own transport? This doesn't just mean do you have a car, but rather; do you have a car that will fit everything in, including me, the kids, the partner, the dog, my lunch, etc. If you need to hire a van, or borrow a car from a family member, then this needs to be taken into consideration at the outset.

What the journey will be like is also worth considering. For your first few fairs, it is likely that it will be local and so you may well know the way. If you are unsure about how to get there, do a recce beforehand or double check on a map. Checking if there are any road works or diversions planned along the route can also save you a panic on the day as can checking local fixtures if you drive past a football or rugby ground.

INDOOR VERSUS OUTDOOR

As a general rule, I would recommend an indoor craft fair for your first taste of the craft fair world. There are pros and cons to each, but indoor fairs somehow feel safer and easier to control when you first start. To be fair, however, I have given you the lowdown on both options.

Outdoor

You are likely to have much more space to spread out.
If you have a gazebo, you can turn it into your own mini shop.

You are more likely to have to supply your own tables.
You may even need to have your own gazebo (and the safety features to anchor it down)
The weather – need I say more. This is the UK after all. You may need suntan lotion and umbrellas all on the same day. The most important one is wind! You need to plan for this carefully.
The wifi signal is often rubbish, especially, I find, in barns ☺
You are likely to have to carry your products and displays across a field. Think about when it goes dark. If it is a Christmas outdoor fair (which can be lovely!), you will want lights on your stall, but you may also need a torch to get back to the car.

Indoor

You will be warm and dry – this counts for a lot!
You will have other stall holders around you to chat with and get to know.
You will generally have a good wifi signal
You may not need Public Liability Insurance for some indoor fairs. You need to check individually.

You will have your designated table space and probably very little extra space to move.
You may boil if you are next to a radiator (maybe this one is just me!?)

Despite all of those things, I would still personally prefer an outdoor fair at any time of year. I may be mad, but I just love the atmosphere you get. You will find what works best for you.

YOUR TURN:

Where do I sell?

It's time for you to make some notes on what you have learned so far. The more information you can record now, the more help it will be later on.

1. Visiting the site   Don't forget to look at Social Media if you can't visit the site in person

Notes on atmosphere, number of stalls, number of customers, signage & advertising, what products are being sold, quality of items etc.

2. Which venues hold craft fairs? e.g. village halls, schools, pubs, retirement villages

Venue name	Distance from home	Notes

3. Indoor or outdoor? pros and cons for me and my situation

Notes:

Planning your table

Right...you are all booked in, confident that the venue will be perfect for you and happy with the products you are going to be selling. Now you need to think about how you are going to display your wares.

This is where it can be easy to come unstuck, but with just a few tweaks, your stall will look professional and inviting and most importantly won't cost a fortune to set up. When you first start, make do with what you already have, rather than splashing out on expensive props.

Let's break it down...

- **HOW MUCH SPACE?**
- **HOW WILL YOU GET THERE?**
- **CREATING HEIGHT ON DISPLAYS**
- **GROUPING ITEMS TOGETHER**
- **SIGNAGE ON THE STALL**

Racecows - 6ft table

HOW MUCH SPACE WILL YOU ACTUALLY HAVE?

Before you can start planning, you of course, need to know how much space you will have on the day. If you are taking your own table, then you can simply put it up at home to practice your layout, but if you are borrowing or hiring a table from the venue, you need to check the sizing and the recreate that space so you can prepare.

I can't reiterate enough, how important it is to practice your layout at home before you sell. Not only will you have the time to try different ideas, but it means that on the day you will know exactly what you are doing, which means less faffing, which means less stress.

If you have been to this event before on a recce, or looked at photos on their Facebook page, then you will also have an idea about how much space you will have between stalls and behind them. It may sound silly, but when stalls are squished together in a long row, getting out to the loo can be a major upheaval.

Do you know if you will have any wall space behind your stall? If so, are you allowed to use this as part of your display? Village halls often have pin boards along their walls and although I would not advise pinning into them, you may be able to hang something on a coat hanger from the top. I have also had instances where I have had a set of coat hooks on the wall behind me. These worked brilliantly for my scarves.

Many venues will send you a floor plan which you use to identify your 'spot' on the day. From this, you can see if you are by an outside door (be aware of things blowing over), on the route to the loo (be aware of not having things sticking out that people might catch on clothing as they walk past), or next to the café (take a big dose of will power ☺)

It should be said, that smaller fairs will still just stick a post-it note on each table and you search for your name when you arrive. Some even have a first come first served arrangement. In this instance, it is worth getting there promptly so you can pick your spot. All of these things should be made clear when you receive your information sheet from the venue. If not, just ask. No one will think any less of you for asking, I promise!

HOW WILL YOU GET THERE?

It sounds obvious, but what will fit into a van, will not fit into a Mini!

Is there going to just be you in the car, or does there need to be room for someone else too? When you are planning your display, just think about the size of your props.

I once bought a fab mesh display stand from eBay. It stood upright at the back of my stall and I could hang things from it. It looked great. The sides came off, as did the feet, so it was 'flat pack'. In my head that was all it needed to be. What I didn't take into account was the mesh itself which may have been flat, but also didn't fold and was 6' by 2'. It fitted in my car. Just. With the passenger side front seat fully forwards. It was an absolute pain to manoeuvre and I ditched it pretty quickly. Don't be a numpty like me; think first!

If you are using props for display (which I recommend), choose things that fold or dismantle. Folding shelves can be very useful where the shelves fold up and the sides fold in. They are not cheap, but if you keep an eye out on your local selling sights, you may pick up a bargain. When I say "things that dismantle", I am not suggesting that you start constructing Ikea furniture or anything like that, but things that slot together, or the base unclicks are really useful. Just be aware of the extra time it will take to set up as well as any allen keys or screwdrivers you may need to take.

Boxes and baskets are your friend when selling at craft fairs. Not only can they be used to display your items, but they double up as the perfect thing to transport your stock in. Wooden crates are very popular for good reason. They are widely available, are solid enough to protect stock on the move and can be used up-side-down or on their side to display your products.

If you are unsure about whether things will fit in the car; try it! Have a go at getting everything in. As you attend more craft fairs, you will find that you gradually work out the best place for everything to go and which order to put it in. It happens without you even thinking about it.

Initially, you just want to make sure that things don't slide around too much as you drive. Old pillows or an old duvet can be really helpful in packing the spaces, especially if your products are breakable and you need them to be stable as you drive. Remember, if you sell lots, your boxes may be quite empty on the way home. This is brilliant, but if you sell large pieces of slate (like we do) it's not too good if they are rattling around.

CREATING HEIGHT ON YOUR DISPLAYS

When you are planning out your stall, you need to think about displaying your items at different heights. Actually, planning out your display is a whole issue in itself and one I'm not going to tackle in great depth here, but there are some basic pointers you need to consider.

I have seen stalls where the seller has simply spread out their products on the table. I remember one instance in particular, where the lady in question simply laid out her coasters in a grid across the whole table. She did not sell anything all day. The rest of the stall holders all tried to offer bits of advice, things to prop up some of the coasters etc, but she was adamant that she didn't need or want our input. At the end of the day, she declared that selling at craft fairs was hopeless and we never saw her again.

Do not be that lady!

Think of your stall as having three distinct levels: tabletop, mid-height and eye level. If possible, you want to have a mixture of all three. Things that work well at table level are pocket money items which will attract children – they always look better on a tray or a shallow bowl than flat on the table; mid height could be something standing on an up-turned crate and eye level is something that will draw the customer in. This works especially well if it is what I call a 'conversation piece' or 'Showstopper'. It may be more expensive or unusual, but often provokes and encourages conversations with customers

Consider where you will be during the fair. Will you be to one side? Behind the table? If you are going to stand behind, then you need to make sure you leave a gap to talk to people. You don't want to be popping up on tiptoes to see your customers. Equally, you need to be accessible to take payment and package up purchases.

A great way to make your stall look cohesive if you have used items from all over is to give them all a lick of paint. If you have various bits of shelving, crates, trays etc that are all mismatched it can look a bit thrown together. Painting them all the same colour brings them together and helps them merge into the background so that it's your products that stand out. Of course you can also go the other way if, for example, vintage is your brand, then covering things in flowery old wallpaper may work brilliantly for you. Being cohesive is the key here.

CREATING COLLECTIONS OF GROUPS OF PRODUCTS

This sounds very grand, but it essentially simply means putting like things together. It is so much less confusing for customers if all the wax melts are together and all the essential oils are together, or if all the rain hats are separate from the bobble hats. You get my drift. You want to make it as easy as possible for your customers to buy from you, so don't try to confuse them! Depending on what you sell, it could be as simple as putting all the items in colours or sizes.

There are several advantages to having things grouped in collections alongside making it easier for the customer to see what you sell and find things if (and when) they come back for more:

- It is so much easier for you to plan out your stall if you group items in 'families'.
- You can see immediately what has sold and what has been most popular.
- You can pack up in an organised way so that getting it all out again at the next fair is easier.
- It makes it very straightforward to sort out your signage and display your pricing.
- It just looks better! ☺

SIGNAGE

Let's look a little more at signage. Firstly, always display your prices. This is hard for some people as they feel uncomfortable doing it, but it is just a fact that customers at fairs and markets do not want to ask for prices and you will absolutely loose sales if you do not have them clearly displayed. There are several ways to price up your items from individual price tags (fiddly and you're guaranteed to miss one) to signs for each collection. I would always advise the latter as it takes less time and you are covered if you need to put out new stock during the sale.

Make sure your signs are easily readable. That beautiful font that you found may look very decorative, but unless it's easy to read from two meters away without reading glasses, then it's not doing you any favours. Signs need to be clear and concise. Think about the colours you use as well as the font.

Making your signs cohesive makes you look much more professional. No matter how you have decided to write your signage, having them all the same is definitely better. When you first start, stiff card folded in half so it stands up like a photo frame is fine. They don't need to be expensive or fancy, they just need to give the customer the information they need in a clear and concise way.

Make any deals that you may have, really clear. Group the items that are covered in the offer together so there is no misunderstanding. Explain on the signage that it is a time sensitive offer. If your customer doesn't take advantage of it today, then they will miss out.

My last piece of advice on signage is to please, please, please check your spelling! If you know that this is a weak point for you; ask someone else to double check for you. Poor spelling looks like you haven't taken the time or care over your stall which means, in the customers mind, that you may not have taken due time and care over the products either.

YOUR TURN:

Planning your table

This time you have quite a bit of work to do! Make sure you try out your different layouts at home on the same sized table you will have on the day of the sale.

1. How large is your space?

   Are there any other considerations? e.g. wall space, on a corner, next to the entrance

2. What have you got already that you could use? e.g. baskets, crates etc

3. How are you going to group your products into collections?

4. Actions grid

Collection name	Optimum display	Equipment used	Height TT/MH/EL
Eco-friendly	Dishcloths - basket Facewipe jars - shelf	vegetable rack folding shelves	TT MH

Table Top
Medium Height
Eye Level

Pre-sale prep

This is where we get down to the practicalities of what you need to do right before you attend your craft fair. As always, some things are more obvious than others, but you would be surprised at how common sense flies out of the window when you are fretting about getting something right or doing something for the first time. It's also true to say that once you have done something a few times, you can get a little blasé and forget something very obvious! I once totally forgot about taking a float and ended running up a very steep hill to the bank with 5 minutes to go before the doors opened. Not ideal, but I have never done it again since!

Ok, let's break it down into manageable chunks...

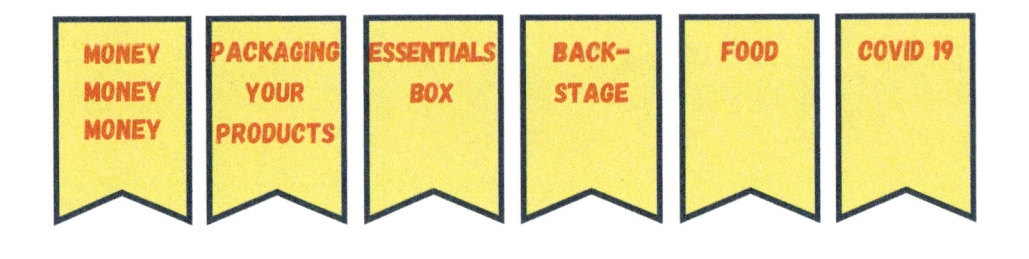

| MONEY MONEY MONEY | PACKAGING YOUR PRODUCTS | ESSENTIALS BOX | BACK-STAGE | FOOD | COVID 19 |

MONEY, MONEY, MONEY

Cash versus card payments. During the Covid pandemic, once face-to-face outdoor events could take place again, cash was often not allowed and at least not encouraged at craft fairs. At my first Market back, I accepted cash, but only if it was the correct amount and I had a money box on the table for the customer to post the payment in. I then left it for a few days before opening. Most people, however, preferred to pay by card. Cash payment has now become more common again, but I would say that around 75% of my customers still prefer to pay by card.

Cash

If you are only accepting cash payments, then you need to make this very clear on your stall. Have a sign to tell people that they need cash. If your items are £10 or below, then people may choose to pay with cash anyway, so it won't be a problem. If you are selling mainly pocket money items to children, then cash is king. If, however, your items are averaging above £15, then you may lose customers if you are not able to accommodate card payments.

Remember my story about not having a float and make sure you nip to the bank a couple of days before your sale. A 'float' is simply the name given to the coins you carry to enable you to give change to your customers.
Do not be tempted to price your items at 99p or 45p etc. People are too savvy these days to think they are cheaper, and you end up with small coins everywhere. Keep it simple – round your prices to a pound or 50p, so that your float only needs to be a few notes (£5 and £10) as well as pound coins and 50 pence pieces. Believe me, you will thank me later!

Card payments

Think about whether this is something you would like to do. Initially, probably not, as you want to 'test the water' and don't want another outlay, but after a few fairs, I would recommend you buying a card reader. There are lots of options out there. You will have heard of SumUp, Square and iZettle to name just three. They all have pros and cons and you need to find one that works for you.

In general:
 PROs:
- It makes it easier for people to pay (got to be good!)
- It may encourage people to spend more (I see this all the time)
- It's very useful if you have high ticket items (products that cost more than £20)

 CONs:
- There is an initial cost to buying the card reader
- You pay a (small) percentage of each transaction to the company
- You are reliant on wifi (most operate through your phone)
- You have to set it up before the sale and check for updates before each sale (sounds tricky, but isn't!)

PACKAGING YOUR PRODUCTS

As ever, I would always recommend keeping this simple to start with. You will find that many people now have their own bags and so do not need one from you, but you need to make sure your items are protected once sold.

Think about what happens once each item is sold. By that, I mean, what physically happens to it. Is it OK to be plopped in the bottom of a bag, or will it need rather more careful handling? If you sell small items, you might find it a good i a to have a small bag ready so that they don't get lost in handbags etc. If you have fragile items, then you may need tissue paper or bubble wrap.

Always go for the most straightforward option. Simple brown or white paper bags are widely available from places such as eBay and Amazon. Make sure you check the sizes carefully before ordering and don't be tempted to buy 500 because they work out cheaper. Once you have tried a few suppliers and you have actually used what they sell you, then is the time to buy in bulk.

You also need to consider the amount of space you need. If you are wrapping items in tissue paper, for example, you may need a flat surface to be able to do that. In that case, a small fold up table could be invaluable to have either behind or to the side of your stall.

Having your bags easily accessible is also important. You don't want customers waiting too long while you try to find the right size. I use a magazine rack for my bags which means they are easy for me to get quickly and easy for me to see all the sizes I have.

You will see people with stamped packaging or with stickers to hold the bag shut at the top. These can look lovely and there are hundreds of places online which will create you a personalised stamp or set of stickers. These may look great, BUT they are not essential. They are fluff. Nice fluff, but still fluff. Coloured tissue paper is more expensive than white. Again, it's lovely if it fits with your branding, but it is fluff. Fluff is where you are aiming. Essential is where you are starting.

FLUFF IS WHERE YOU ARE AIMING

ESSENTIAL IS WHERE YOU ARE STARTING

ESSENTIALS BOX

This is SO important. It could be a basket or a bag, but whatever you use, you NEED to have one and you need it to be accessible. This is the place where you have your safety pins, blue tack, pens, scissors, card reader, tape, chalk, spare batteries, notebook, screwdriver, allen keys... basically anything and everything that you may need on your stall. This is such a vital piece of kit that it deserves its own section. Keep everything in one place and when you use something, put it back in.

If you do nothing else, do this.

BACKSTAGE

I mentioned the back of your stall in an earlier chapter and now you will see why it is so important. The most important thing (and something that many craft fairs insist on) is having a tablecloth that reaches to the floor at the front and sides. A simple white bed sheet is the easiest option, and still, in my view, one of the best. Having a white background for your items makes the products stand out. Make sure to safety pin the corners so that there are no dangling folds of material for people (including you!) to trip over, though.

Having a cloth that covers your stall to the floor on all three sides that the customer can see, means that you will have a tidy and professional looking stall. You can use the under-table area to store any extra stock, boxes, packaging etc. You need to make sure that the items you will need (such as packaging) are nearest to you, but you can hide just about anything under a craft stall 😊

Having a designated 'somewhere' to keep your card reader, if you have one, and your phone is a good idea too. If you are using a set of shelves on an angle, the triangle behind that is a perfect place. It is dead space as far as your stall goes; cannot be seen by the customer; and has easy access for you when you need it.

FOOD

If you are going to be at a craft fair all day, food is important to consider. Remember, the craft fair may only be 3 hours long, but with the set up, packing away and transport times to add on, you will probably need 'something to keep you going' as my Nan used to say. Be organised and plan your strategy before the day.

It is likely that there will be some food available at the craft fair. Often it smells lovely and looks yummy. Decide before you go if you are going to give in and buy. Keep in mind that anything you spend on food is taking away from your profits for the day. I would suggest always taking something with you so you can resist spending money while you are there. If you absolutely have to have one of the chocolate brownies that are right in front of you all day, then make a pact with yourself not to buy anything until you have made at least the same amount on your stall. Be strong! It is incredibly easy to spend more on lunch than you take all afternoon.

Drinks are very important. I always take a flask of tea as well as a bottle of water. If you are doing lots of talking (which we hope you will be), you will need plenty to drink.

It is one of the unwritten Laws of the Universe that the way to make someone ask you a question is to take a big bite of food. If the room is empty and you grab a bite of your sandwich, it is guaranteed that someone will appear out of nowhere to ask for clarification on your prices. To help with this, choose easy food. By that, I mean, food that is easy to pick up and put down. A sandwich is good, a yoghurt can be tricky. Also choose something that won't make a mess on you or your table. Flaky pastry is best avoided ☺

COVID 19

Unfortunately, it appears Covid 19 is here to stay and so needs a quick mention in this section. Before attending any fairs, you need to be up to date on what the Government guidance is at that time and in the country where the event is taking place. Be particularly aware if you are crossing the Welsh or Scottish borders with England, as the guidance may be different.

The organisation running the event may also have rules about what they would expect stall holders to do or provide. It is your responsibility to make sure you are following the rules. You will not be able to say later that you didn't know, if it is in the information pack.

As I can't see into the future (nor would I want to!), I have no idea if this guidance would now apply to other viruses or pandemics. I am assuming you will use your common sense on this one.

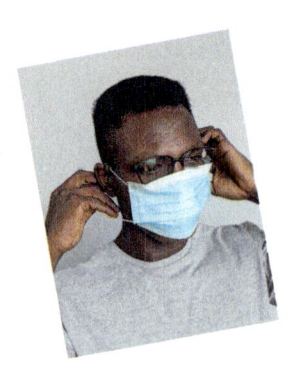

YOUR TURN:
Pre-sale Prep

The more you do now, the easier it will be on the day of your craft fair. Stick with it and plan ahead.

1. Cash float - only you can work this out based on your prices.

I have given you an example of what I use, just as an idea. Record yours below and review it after your first fair.

£20 notes	£10 notes	£5 notes	£1 coins	50p coins	Total
1	*2*	*4*	*10*	*10*	*£95*

Card reader - if using. I will set time aside to set this up on:

2. Packaging

Provider	Sizes available	Cost per bag (Total cost divided by quantity)	Quantity	Total cost
Amazon	*5"x9"x3.5"*	*20p*	*50*	*£10.05*

1

3. Essentials box/bag checklist I have just started you off, add your own items to the list

- [ ] Pens
- [ ] Notebook
- [ ] Blu Tack
- [ ] Sellotape and/or washi tape
- [ ] Safety pins
- [ ] Screwdriver
- [ ] Allen key
- [ ] Chalk
- [ ] Blank price tags/signs
- [ ] Deodorant
- [ ] Mints
- [ ] Lipstick
- [ ]
- [ ]
- [ ]
- [ ]
- [ ]
- [ ]
- [ ]
- [ ]
- [ ]
- [ ]
- [ ]
- [ ]
- [ ]

4. Main checklist Add or delete as necessary

- [ ] Table
- [ ] Chair
- [ ] Float
- [ ] Card reader
- [ ] Mobile phone
- [ ] Essentials box/bag
- [ ] Table cloth(s)
- [ ] Products
- [ ] Signs
- [ ] Display furniture
- [ ] Packaging
- [ ] Food
- [ ] Drink
- [ ] Extra jumper/coat
- [ ]
- [ ]
- [ ]
- [ ]
- [ ]
- [ ]
- [ ]
- [ ]
- [ ]
- [ ]

On the day!

So, you have finally got to the day of the sale, and you are all ready to go. Now we get to the nitty gritty (technical term) of your craft fair experience. As always, there are a few things to be aware of which are worth thinking about before hand.

This is, as ever, just a brief overview of the day. There are several aspects which I could go into in much more detail, but this is not the place for that. If you are a shy person, for example; look out for my Top Tips for Shy Sellers.

The topics covered in this chapter are:

WILL YOU BE ALONE?	ACCESS ISSUES	WHAT TO WEAR
TALK TO THE STALLHOLDERS	TALKING TO CUSTOMERS	KEEP A LIST OF SALES

WILL YOU BE ALONE?

This is a key factor. I think it is always good to have an extra body along for your first fair at least, although you do have had to make sure that they will fit in the packed car!

Having an extra pair of hands can really help when unloading and setting up your stall. You may need to give them specific jobs to do, but even having someone to just get products out of boxes for you can be a huge help. Having someone available to help with your unpacking and then reloading at the end, can be invaluable.

If your helper is going to stay for the whole sale, you need to make sure that they are aware of prices and any deals as well as possibly how to work a card reader. Alternatively, they may decide that they are simply there as moral support, and you do all the interactions with customers.

The most important thing to remember if you are on your own on your stall, is to go to the loo before the doors open to the public. It may sound amusing, but I can assure you it's not funny, if you get stuck without being able to get out from behind your stall in a packed hall!

Having an extra pair of hands to help you unload the car is always welcome!

ACCESS ISSUES

Hopefully you will have been able to suss this out before the actual day, so will be able to plan ahead.

Many venues have their own parking, but you are often asked to park elsewhere once you have unloaded so that customers can park nearer the entrance. Some places may not have their own parking at all and you will need to find a local car park. You will need to check on the parking situation. Find out how close the nearest parking is. If it is Pay and Display, make sure you have the correct coins if necessary (in many villages, you will still need coins) and find out how far it is from the Craft Fair. If you have a helper on the day that can drive, they can disappear off with the car for you, but if you are on your own, you will need to have time to go and park, and then walk back to the hall before you can start setting up.

Knowing if you are on the ground floor or upstairs is useful. It can definitely influence how you pack your items. If you have to carry all your products up a steep flight of stairs as there is no lift, you would probably choose to pack fewer heavy things together. If you are a distance from the nearest parking, but the route is not too uneven, would a small cart be useful? This is often worth considering when (if) you progress to larger venues outside where you may be transporting a gazebo across a field, for example.

Always find out the earliest time you are able to set up. When you are starting out at craft fairs, try to get there as early as you can.

It is always better to have 10 minutes before the doors are opened where you are just waiting, rather than panicking that you won't have everything ready in time.

WHAT TO WEAR

This is pretty much common sense, but all boils down to one word – layers! You will find that unpacking and carting stuff about (that's a technical term for setting up your stall), alongside fretting about the time, whether you have forgotten anything and how it will all look, will make you hot and flustered. Once you stop, however, it can be a different story. You will probably not know until the day if you will be right next to a huge radiator or directly in line with the draft from the outside door. Layers are your friend.

You need to look smart when on your stall. This seems obvious, but if you have something that can be messy to set up, taking an extra top is a good idea. I have a friend that uses straw bales as part of her display of goat's milk soaps. It looks great, but the straw tends to get everywhere when she is setting up in a morning. She always brings a spare top and does a quick change in the loo before the doors open to the public.

If you make any form of clothing or accessories – wear one!! I never understand people who don't do this. Customers want to see how it looks on. If you sell hats and you are wearing one, you will be spotted from across the hall. As a side note here: make a decision about people trying on your items. If you are happy for people to try on, then make sure you have a mirror handy, if you are not comfortable with that (or regulations at the time don't allow it), then make that clear to your customers.

TALK TO THE OTHER STALLHOLDERS

I have covered this in previous chapters, but it is worth repeating. The information and experience of other stall holders is worth it's weight in gold. Be friendly and chat if and when you can. This is by far the best way to find out about other fairs which may suit you. It will also be noted by the organisers and you will be welcomed back 😊

Make a note of other stallholders and their business names. If they are local, it can be good to follow them and tag them on social media. They will do the same for you.

TALKING TO CUSTOMERS

I could write a whole book about just this section (and maybe I will ☺), but this is the key to success. It is also the aspect of fairs that many people find the most difficult. If you are a naturally shy person, this can seem very awkward and uncomfortable. My best advice to you would be to put on a persona for the day. Act as though you are confident and happy to chat. As they say these days (how old do I sound!?) 'Fake it 'til you make it'. Here are a few quick tips to get you through:

- ALWAYS smile at each person that walks past and say 'Hi' or 'Morning'. Some people will ignore you – that's fine. They are just shy and uncomfortable too. Let it go. Most people will smile back and return your greeting. Great. They are left with a feeling that you are friendly and not pushy. They may well come back. Some people will stop and look more closely at your products. They are your customers and the ones you want to engage with. What you need to remember is that greeting EVERYONE can turn the shy, unsure person into the interested customer.

- You don't just have to talk about your products. Complementing someone on their choice of earrings or the colour of their scarf; sympathising that they got caught in the heavy shower as they arrived; or recommending the amazing homemade cakes in the café are all great ways to start a conversation. That may be as far as it goes. That's fine. You will have been noted by that customer as a friendly and approachable person which is always a good thing. For some people, however, it will lead on to a discussion about what you sell.

- If you are asked about your products or you notice someone is particularly interested in something, give them a little bit of background. Letting people know a little about what goes into making that product helps them to see the value of it. That could mean what goes into it in terms of ingredients (think lavender and camomile or homespun wool) or it could mean what goes into it in terms of time and effort (think 'each one takes me about 6 hours to complete'). You can also ask questions such as 'Which is your favourite?' 'I'm trying to work out which colour combination works best, what do you think?' This directly involves the customer in your thought process and makes them much more likely to buy.

- If you are so shy that the idea of starting a conversation is causing you to wonder whether you actually want to do this whole craft fair thing or not, then never fear! You do have to smile at each person, but you can make sure you take something to work on while you are sitting there. This is then a great conversation starter in itself, and you are getting something done at the same time! Just please, please, please, please do not be one of those people who sit and *knit* (*insert your craft here) behind their stall all day and simply ignore everything and everyone around them and then complain when they have sold next to nothing!

- One thing that I will mention here, is handling negative comments. You will almost definitely have someone who thinks your prices are too high, or they could make the same things themselves. In this situation, you have to simply smile and let them move on. They are not your customers and they are entitled to their opinion. Don't rise to it and don't let it get you down. Focus on the positive comments instead.

KEEP A LIST OF SALES

As you sell each item on the day – make a note of it. Some people like to have a notebook handy and some just make a list on a scrap of paper or a paper bag. Whichever works for you, you will be glad that you did. If you have an offer – for example, £7 each or two for £10, make sure you make a note of that too. It's a good idea to keep tabs on which colour or scent has been sold. If you have a stock list, you can work this out later, but if not, just a quick note will remind you later.

The most important thing to remember about your day is to enjoy it!

Yes, you are hoping to sell lots of stock, but first and foremost you need to have fun. Take the pressure and expectations away and chat to people, watch other sellers and make your own mind up about what works and what doesn't.

YOUR TURN:
On the day!

Let's make sure that the day itself goes as smoothly as possible and you get to actually enjoy it!!

1. Who is able to help on the day?

What do they need to know beforehand? e.g. how to use the card reader

2. Access

Where can I park?

Do I need to pay for parking? How much?

How far away is the parking? How long will it take me to walk there?

What is the earliest time I can start setting up?

What time do the doors open to customers?

What time does the fair finish?

3. Items I want to remember to wear on the day are:

Remember to wear things that you make if you can.

4. Projects I could take with me on the day:

This is easier for some than others. If your skill is not something easy to transport like knitting, then could you take some preparation 'jobs' such as folding packaging. Remember, you don't HAVE to take something to do, you can just chat!

After your craft fair

The fair is over and the doors have closed. Now you have to pack everything away and go home and decide if you ever want to go through it again ☺

As ever, I have a few thoughts and pointers to help with this last stage of your craft market. You may as well keep reading – you've got this far after all!!

You may have noticed - much of the work of craft fairs involves packing - packing up, packing away, unpacking....it just goes on...

Here we will thing about **PACKING AWAY**

Then we will consider the worst bit **UNPACKING AT HOME**

Before finally looking at **THREE IMPORTANT THINGS TO DO OVER A CUPPA**

PACKING AWAY

You will often notice that some stall holders start to pack away before the end of the fair. You will also probably have seen that the organisers have explicitly asked you not to do this. It is true that some fairs are unfortunately like the Marie Celeste and are deathly quiet for the last half hour. The temptation to pack away early is strong. I think there are two very good reasons why you should not be the one doing this.

Firstly, it tells the organisers that you are not concerned about their rules. If you never want to go back, then ok, I suppose, but the crafting world is a small one and I have had many conversations over the years with stall holders who say things like "I had two soap makers apply for a table. I gave it to *** because I heard that the other one always packs away early" The last thing that organisers want it to have bare tables before the end of the fair.

The second reason for not packing away early is that you may still sell! I have always taken the view that I was planning for the market to last x number of hours, so that's how long I will stay. There is always a crush to get out of the car park anyway, so you may as well take a little time. I regularly sell items in the last half hour (especially before Christmas) when others are packing away as my stall still looks inviting and I am relaxed and friendly.

Another good reason for taking a calm and measured approach to packing away is so you pack everything up safely and so you know where it is. When you get home, the first thing you will want to do is put the kettle on. You will not want to get everything out again to pack it up properly.

Think about how you packed to go to the fair and just do the same in reverse. It may sound obvious now, but the temptation to just chuck thinks in boxes willy nilly is strong when your feet ache and you need to get home in time to make dinner. Fight the urge! It really is worth that couple of extra minutes.

If you have a helper, they can be a life saver when packing up. I know that the sight of my hubby striding across the barn after a market is a huge relief as we have packed up hundreds of times before and we just slot into our 'jobs' and the car gets packed in record time. This may not be the case when you are first starting out – it certainly wasn't for me. It can help to have designated jobs for the helper to do. For example, I always pack the items into the boxes and crates and then Dave packs the crates into the car. He could have a good go at packing up the products (I would probably re-do it later – rather like the dishwasher!) and I can pack the car, but we have been doing it for a while now and each of us is an expert in our own part of the packing process. Make life easy on yourselves. You don't want to end your day by getting frustrated now, just because you're tired.

Don't let the tiredness monster win now. Just one last push and you can have your well deserved cuppa (and count up all your takings!)

UNPACKING AT HOME

This is hands down the worst bit of any fair or market for me. I hate it. When I get home, all I want to do is put the kettle on and have a cuppa, but instead I'm faced with a car full of stuff that not only needs to be emptied, but needs to be put away as well. For me, it has to be an immediate job. If I sat down with a cuppa at that point, I would never get the car unloaded! I put the kettle on, so there is the promise of a brew on the way, and then I tackle the car. If you have packed up with some thought at the venue, this is easier than it would otherwise be.

If you can, move boxes and crates straight from the car to where they 'live' at home. If that isn't possible straight away (because you need to empty a box etc), then at least put it in the correct room. The more you can do with that last burst of energy, the better. You might find that you are not particularly tired, but if you have been standing and chatting for several hours to strangers, then you should be at least a little weary.

When packing things away, try to keep them grouped in their collections. This makes them much easier to find if you need to work on them, check stock, replace items and so on. Boxes with labels are also brilliant here. I am sure you have your craft stocks all neatly labelled ☺ but having things labelled for selling finished products is a slightly different thing than having the 'raw ingredients' labelled. It can also be handy to have a note on the box that you can add to. For example, if you have a few sizes of bells, having one jar with 'Elf hats' added to the label can save time trying to work out what you used last year.

THREE IMPORTANT THINGS TO DO OVER A CUPPA

Once you have your cuppa in hand, or any other beverage, for that matter, there are just three things left to do...

1. Make some notes about the venue

- Would you sell there again? If not, why not? You will come back and read this in, perhaps a year's time, so be precise. If there is one thing that put you off (such as lack of advertising), it may be that new organisers have taken it over and you can ask about that aspect before you sign up.

- What was especially good or bad for you specifically? If you had a corner table and being able to have some items at the side worked well, note it down. If you had a corner table and you found that people kept knocking your display as they walked round, note that down too. Having coat hooks behind your stall could be brilliant for you to hang products and add to your display space or it could be very painful as they are just at head height, and you find you are getting up and down all day. When you can identify things that work well or badly for you, you can look to replicate or avoid them at other venues.

2. Note down recurring comments or questions

- You will find that there are a few things that you feel like you have said hundreds of times over the afternoon. Some of these will be good conversation starters and worth remembering. You will also have to live with the fact that you keep repeating yourself – the trick is to say it each time like you've never said it before ☺

- If there are questions or comments about your products that have given you ideas for new products – make a note. You need to avoid falling down the rabbit hole here, though. Just because two people have asked about Jasmine scented candles does not necessarily mean that it would be a great idea to start making them. Don't get me wrong, it *could* be a great idea, but you need to decide that with your rational business head on later.

- If there are questions that you have answered over and over, think about how you could get that information to people without them having to ask. You can guarantee that for every person who has asked, there are more who have thought it, but not wanted to ask to find out the answer. Is it worth writing a sign? Is it something that you could make clear on your packaging?

- You will find that you tend to focus on any negative comments – it's just human nature. They may not actually be negative, but you perceive them as such. If you hear "Oh, hello! I didn't see you behind there!" more than a couple of times, then it may be time to re-think your display slightly. I would definitely recommend keeping a list of all the lovely things people say to you. "Oh, those colours are pretty"; "Ooooh, this is so beautifully soft"; "Gosh you are clever, this must have taken hours" These comments are the ones you need to hold on to the most. Write them in a little book and get it out to read it every time you wonder if you are mad to be doing this craft thing.

3. Keep a record of your sales

- You will (hopefully) have a list from your craft fair of what you sold. You can now use this to look at what sold well, what sold a little and what didn't sell at all. You will need several fairs under your belt before you can start to see the trends. What sells well in one venue, may not in another. Equally, what sells well one week may not then sell at all for the next two sales. There is often no rhyme or reason to it. Just accept that it happens and look at the bigger picture.

- You will need your list to know what stock needs to be replaced before your next fair. It is useful to look at any offers you had too. If you had a two for one offer, and each time a customer chose two scents, one was mint, then it is pretty obvious that you need to make more mint items than other scents for the future.

- The easiest way to record your sales is on a simple spreadsheet. This could be electronically (a very simple Excel spreadsheet is very straightforward) or just old-school in a notebook. At this stage, you will probably not be thinking about having to pay tax as you will not be making anywhere near the threshold, but it is a good practice to get into. All you need to do is keep a list with the date, item name, number sold, and price. This also gets you into the head space of running a small business, which may be slightly scary, but is also very exciting!

YOUR TURN:

After your craft fair

You did it!! Well done! Hopefully you had a great time and chatted to lots of people whilst making sales - that's what it's all about after all. Now finish off strong and you will be ahead of the game for the next one!

1. Things to think about to help me pack away more easily...

At the fair...   At home...

2. Recurring questions/ comments

Comment/ question   Action needed (if any)

3. Venue notes

Venue name and location _____

Good	Not so good!

Contact name _____
Contact email/phone number _____

4. Record of sales

Item	Number sold & how	Total sale
Market bag	3 sold individually @ £12 2 sold as part of deal @ £8	3 × 12 = £36 2 × 8 = £16

Total sales: £

So there you have it...

My top tips for being a successful craft fair seller right from the start.

I can't promise that if you follow all of my ideas, you will be an overnight success, but I can promise that you will be better prepared and more aware than most people starting out (and a few who have been selling for a while too!)

Always remember that this is supposed to be fun. Keep everything in perspective and just enjoy yourself. People are more likely to buy from a smiling face.

If you would like to join our friendly and supportive group of crafters, pop over to my Facebook Group:

CRAFT MARKET MASTERS

We are a great community of people just like you. It is where I share top tips, seasonal ideas, answer questions and more. Hope to see you there!

Printed in Great Britain
by Amazon